Australia In Focus

AUSTRALIA

CONTENTS

Page 1: Whispering palms on a crisp sandy beach, sailcraft on a peacock-blue ocean – hallmarks of the Whitsundays. *Page 2–3:* The Rock, Uluru, in brilliant red at twilight. *Opposite:* The Great Barrier Reef teems with colourful marine life.

INTRODUCTION

Australia is a vast island continent of remarkable natural and cultural diversity. The intriguing history of its evolution is evident in the subtle beauty of its weathered landscapes and in its unique native plants and animals. Australia's human history reaches back some 60,000 years when people first began arriving on its northern coastlines. Today its culturally diverse cities continue to draw citizens from around the world.

This book brings into focus some of my favourite images of our great southern land and its people. I spend as much time as I can wandering Australia's highways and byways in search of new places and sights to record on film and I never tire of the beauty that confronts me at every turn. I hope you enjoy this visual celebration of Australia and are inspired to embark on your own journey of discovery.

Steve Parish

Left: *Sydney Harbour Bridge frames the soaring skyline of the Sydney Opera House.* **Right:** *Michael Jagamara Nelson's intricate mosaic graces the Forecourt of the Australian Parliament House, Canberra.*

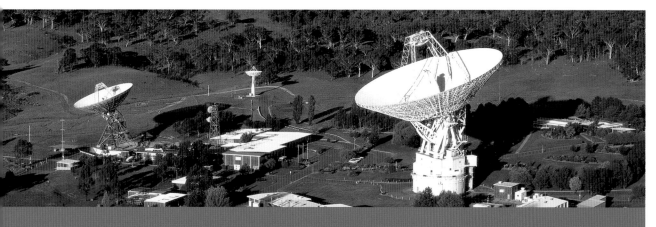

AUSTRALIAN CAPITAL TERRITORY

The Australian Capital Territory is home to the nation's capital city, Canberra. It lies midway between Sydney and Melbourne on an undulating limestone plain beneath the north-eastern slopes of the Australian Alps.

Plans for the national capital began in 1901 with the Federation of the States of Australia and continued with the establishment of the ACT in 1911. Since the striking of the first survey peg in 1913, Canberra has evolved into a gracious city and a worthy domain for the Australian Federal Parliament and Australia's national institutions.

The success of Canberra as a planned city owes much to the architectural vision of Walter Burley Griffin, who championed the union of landscape and architecture. The thoughtful integration of Canberra's built environment with its natural features has created a spacious city, with the Parliamentary Triangle on the southern shores of Lake Burley Griffin. At its heart, Parliament House on Capital Hill is the focal point of the many government and cultural institutions that lie within the triangle.

Stately, tree-lined avenues radiate from this political hub to the leafy suburbs. More than half of the ACT is set aside as national parks and nature reserves that encompass natural bushland, mountain ranges and rivers. These conservation areas, along with Canberra's formal parks and gardens, offer residents and visitors many opportunities for relaxation and outdoor leisure activities.

Opposite: *A spectacular way to see Parliament House and Old Parliament House is by hot air balloon.* **This page:** *The Deep Space Communication Complex at Tidbinbilla receives and transmits commands from deep space.*

CANBERRA

Canberra, named for a Ngunnawal word for "meeting place", is an attractive, well planned city that takes pride in its role as the national capital. Its temperate climate and landscaped setting provide an ever-changing backdrop of seasonal colours for the city's many public buildings and gracious monuments.

Above, clockwise from top left: The Canberra Centre in Civic; ANZAC Parade; an aerial view of Telstra Tower and Civic; a hot air balloon rises over the National Museum of Australia. *Left:* A view across Canberra to the Brindabella Ranges beyond.

DISCOVERING CANBERRA

An incredible variety of public attractions offer locals and visitors insights into the nation's past, present and future. Institutions such as the National Dinosaur Museum, the Australian National Botanic Gardens, and the Australian War Memorial are all within easy reach of the city centre and showcase Australia's diverse natural and cultural heritage.

This page, clockwise from top: The tranquillity of the Australian National Botanic Gardens; discovering the past at the National Dinosaur Museum; the Australian War Memorial. Opposite, top to bottom: Sailing on Lake Burley Griffin; Floriade, Australia's Celebration of Spring brings an extravaganza of colour to Commonwealth Park.

NEW SOUTH WALES

New South Wales is the founding State of modern Australia and is Australia's most populous State. The colony of New South Wales was founded on 26 January 1788 as a British penal settlement. The promise of a new life and a wealth of untapped natural resources attracted free settlers to the fledgling colony and settlement soon spread beyond the sheltered shores of Sydney Harbour.

The State occupies about ten percent of the continent. Most of its southern boundary is marked by the mighty Murray River. To the east, the temperate waters of the Pacific Ocean bathe its long coastline. Inland from its narrow coastal plains, the countryside rises steeply to the peaks and highlands of the Great Dividing Range then slopes across the western plains to the outback aridlands.

New South Wales and its residents enjoy a high standard of living. While natural resources and primary production remain the foundations of the State's prosperity, New South Wales is a leader in the manufacturing, finance, service and technology industries.

New South Wales is also rich in scenic wonders. Between its sculpted seashores and desert dunes is a world of ephemeral wetlands, alpine meadows, mist-shrouded escarpments and subtropical rainforests. Many of these spectacular natural landscapes are protected by the State's extensive system of national parks and reserves.

With its diversity of cities, towns and wild places, New South Wales has much to offer as a holiday destination and as a place to live.

*This page: Locals and visitors enjoy soaking up the sun on Bondi Beach. **Opposite:** Surf Lifesaving Club members hone their skills.*

SYDNEY – THE HARBOUR CITY

Sydney, the capital of New South Wales is a vibrant and sophisticated metropolis blessed with a mild climate and a magnificent harbourside setting.

Australia's most recognised and celebrated icons, the Sydney Opera House and Harbour Bridge, are the true jewels in Sydney's tourism crown. Year round, these spectacular feats of architecture draw crowds of sightseers and tourists. The awe-inspiring steel structure of the Sydney Harbour Bridge connects Sydney with the city's leafy North Shore and represents an important transport link for the city. The Opera House is characterised by its maritime-themed sails – massive shells perching dramatically on top of the performance halls in imitation of the billowing sails of boats on the harbour. Life in Sydney centres on the harbour and these features make it arguably the most famous harbour in the world.

Above: An eastern view across Double Bay and Rose Bay to Watson's Bay. *Left:* Sailors enjoy the harbour playground. *Opposite, top to bottom:* The dramatic Sydney Opera House is recognised worldwide; Sydney Harbour Bridge.

SYDNEY'S WATERFRONT

Life in Sydney is lived on the waterfront and many of the city's major attractions are situated there, including Taronga Zoo, the Royal Botanic Gardens, the Opera House, Luna Park, and, of course, the superb beaches. Surfing and sailing are popular pastimes for many Sydney residents, but the less adventurous can simply watch a magnificent cruise ship, flanked by a multitude of smaller vessels, sail through the heads into Circular Quay or take their own cruise on the Manly Ferry. Some of the city's most celebrated entertainment precincts are also based on the waterfront. Darling Harbour is the most well-known and comes alive with busy eateries and laser shows at night.

Opposite page, top to bottom: Manly Beach fronts the Pacific Ocean; aerial view of the heads at the entrance to Sydney Harbour. **This page top to bottom:** The Manly Ferry takes sightseers into Circular Quay; Maroubra Beach.

THE BLUE MOUNTAINS

The Blue Mountains, 65 kilometres west of Sydney, are an impressive maze of sandstone escarpments and deep river valleys. The region is centred on the township of Katoomba, where the area's most noted landmark – the Three Sisters, a stark rocky outcrop at Echo Point – is located. Stunning views of these rock sentinels can be had from the Scenic Skyway and Scenic Flyway, two chairlift-style transporters over the steep hills and valleys. First settled as a mountain retreat for wealthy Sydneysiders, this area is now famous for its national parks, native wildlife, charming towns and splendid gardens. The wide-open spaces, fresh air and crisp climate of the mountains provide the perfect natural foil to the city's bustle.

Clockwise from above left: Historic Yester-Grange at Wentworth Falls; autumn's colours transform a garden in the Blue Mountains. Opposite: The Scenic Skyway cable car gives stunning views of the Three Sisters and Jamison Valley.

AROUND THE CENTRAL COAST

Past the wide, watery expanse of Broken Bay, Pittwater and the Hawkesbury River, north of Sydney, is the lush New South Wales Central Coast. Beautiful bays and beaches, as well as pockets of wilderness and national park, dot the coast or burst in brilliant greenery from the undulating hills of the hinterland.

On the coast, past the beaches of Avoca and Terrigal, are The Entrance, Wyong, Toukley and other towns scattered around two massive lakes: Tuggerah and Macquarie. These towns follow a string of secluded beaches and inlets up to the city of Newcastle – Australia's sixth-largest city and the industrial hub of the State. Inland are the rolling dales and sleepy towns of the lower Hunter Valley, renowned for its fine wines and thoroughbred horses.

Top to bottom: *Tomaree Head overlooks Port Stephens; the Hunter Valley is a wine connoisseur's paradise; fishing along the Central Coast; Nobbys Beach, Newcastle.*

THE NORTH COAST

The North Coast is a popular destination for holiday-makers and those seeking an alternative to city life. Behind its beaches and charming towns, river tributaries cascade through rainforest gullies on the Great Dividing Range.

Newcastle is a major regional centre with a well respected university, a vibrant arts scene and a proud history. The central business district is close to Newcastle Beach and the Hunter River, reinforcing the city's strong links with the sea. North of the busy industry and workaday world of Newcastle, is Port Stephens – a picturesque spot with sandy, sun-drenched shores overlooked by the dramatic rocky outcrop of Tomaree Head. Travelling through Port Macquarie, and on to Coffs Harbour, visitors find an attractive tourist strip with beaches, mountains and dense rainforest all close by.

Above: Coffs Harbour is a sheltered haven for fishing vessels and pleasure craft. Left: The Solitary Islands, including South Solitary, are renowned for their marine life.

THE FAR WEST

This is the land of outback legends where hope and endurance overcome the isolation and harsh conditions. Water is scarce, but when rain falls desert soils blossom with flowers and wildlife flocks to once dry riverbeds and waterholes. Broken Hill, one of the world's great mining centres is located 1158 kilometres west of Sydney, so far west it operates on South Australian time. Other mining towns in the Outback include Bourke, Cobar and Lightning Ridge, the principle opal-mining town.

Clockwise from top left: Argent Street in the mining town of Broken Hill; Silverton's rich heritage buildings, such as the Municipal Chambers building (1889), attract artists and film-makers; Red Kangaroos are a common sight in western New South Wales; outback flora is adapted to long droughts.

FROM PLAINS TO RANGE

The rolling western plains comprise some of Australia's best pastoral and agricultural country. Plains rise to the Great Dividing Range, where the eroded remains of ancient volcanoes create dramatic landscapes.

Western Plains Zoo, near Dubbo, provides a home for more than 1000 exotic and native animals in open exhibits. With concealed moats separating the animals from human observers, visitors can enjoy watching the animals roam as they would in the wild. Since opening in 1977, the zoo has developed a reputation as a world-renowned centre for wildlife care, conservation programs, breeding programs (especially of endangered species), educational facilities and exhibits.

Clockwise from top left: The architecture of a bygone era at Hill End; Giraffes peer from their open enclosure at Western Plains Zoo; the sheer volcanic plugs in Warrumbungle National Park beckon daring bushwalkers and rock climbers.

Wollongong

Coal-seams of the Illawarra escarpment are the lifeblood of Wollongong and Port Kembla, which are famous for their steel and shipping industries. Wollongong's proud maritime history is commemorated at historic Flagstaff Point, but smaller vessels also played their part in the city's growth, with Belmore Basin sheltering the multitude of fishing boats that comprise a thriving commercial fishing industry.

The city's burgeoning cultural scene is enhanced by the university, botanic gardens, art gallery, science centre and Conservatorium of Music. "The Gong", as the locals call it, is also home to the Nan Tien Buddhist Temple, the largest Buddhist temple in the Southern Hemisphere. The temple was founded in 1965 and its name *Nan Tien* literally means "Paradise of the South".

Clockwise from left: Wollongong Harbour's first lighthouse, at Belmore Basin, began operating in 1872; fishermen unload their catch at Wollongong; the Nan Tien Buddhist Temple.

SOUTHERN HIGHLANDS

The highlands sit atop a mass of sandstone carved by the Shoalhaven and Kangaroo Rivers, which tumble into the valleys below in a number of spectacular cascades. The wilderness areas of Budderoo National Park and the rugged Morton National Park, with its mountainous Budawang Ranges, provide habitat for Eastern Grey Kangaroos, Swamp Wallabies and many species of birds and reptiles. Nearby, pretty Kangaroo Valley can by accessed by the historic Hamden Bridge, a grand castellated structure built in 1897.

Clockwise from above: The Waratah is New South Wales' floral emblem; Hampden Bridge in Kangaroo Valley; Carrington Falls, Budderoo National Park.

SOUTH COAST

Between the calm waters of Jervis Bay and the open sea off Cape Howe is a coastal wonderland. Offshore, in the Tasman Sea, countless fish and invertebrates make their home along the coast from Jervis Bay to Merimbula. Inland, quiet, pretty towns and villages are renowned for their quality produce.

Clockwise from top left: Eden; the country charm of Tilba; Eastern Grey Kangaroos graze by a secluded bay; the blue waters of Merimbula's lagoon, lakes and ocean lap the white sand fringed with bushland.

THE NEW SOUTH WALES ALPS

Mt Kosciuszko, at 2228 metres, crowns the foothills, high plains and granite peaks of the State's magnificent alpine country. The many aspects of its untamed beauty are revealed with the changing of the seasons. In spring, the Alps are carpeted with wildflowers; in winter, they wear a dense blanket of snow.

Clockwise from top: A white-cloaked Snow Gum woodland; colourful wildflowers are a highlight of summer bushwalks; ancient and gnarled Snow Gums edge the alpine meadows.

QUEENSLAND

Queensland, Australia's second-largest State, extends across 1, 728, 000 square kilometres and contains diverse landscapes and climatic zones.

Prior to European settlement, Aboriginal people inhabited the north-eastern part of the continent, and rock art sites around the State are reminders of age-old cultural traditions.

The British colonial era began in Queensland with the establishment of a penal outpost at Moreton Bay in 1824 and ended with self-governance in 1859, when Brisbane officially became the State's capital. Brisbane has matured into a thriving commercial and administrative centre where the warmth and almost year-round sunshine encourage an outdoor lifestyle.

Queensland's population is concentrated along a narrow eastern seaboard famed for its beaches, rainforests, reefs, cays and continental islands. The coral ramparts of the Great Barrier Reef protect most of the coastal plains from the waves of the Pacific Ocean.

Beyond the forested slopes and peaks of the Great Dividing Range lies the magic of the west. This is frontier country, where savannah-clad tablelands and grassy plains give way to the inland floodplains of the Channel Country and ranks of rust-coloured dunes stretching to the heart of Australia.

Today, the Sunshine State is Australia's favourite holiday destination with millions of tourists each year experiencing Queensland's myriad attractions and enjoying the idyllic weather that the State's motto describes as "Beautiful one day, perfect the next".

This page: Crystal-clear water meets lush rainforest on Muggy Muggy Beach, Dunk Island. Opposite: Hinchinbrook Island, part of the Wet Tropics World Heritage Area.

BRISBANE

Brisbane, the capital of Queensland, has the largest metropolitan area of any Australian city. With a population nearing two million, the city spreads along a coastal plain, bordered to the east by the shallow waters of Moreton Bay and by the forested slopes of the D'Aguilar Range to the west. The city itself is bisected by the broad reaches of the meandering Brisbane River, which reflects a friendly, cosmopolitan city that makes the most of its subtropical climate. Alfresco dining, riverside promenades, leafy suburbs and shady verandahs are all part of the city's relaxed style, with residents enjoying the benefits of Brisbane's waterways and parklands throughout Queensland's mild winters and sultry summers.

This page: The Brisbane River loops around South Brisbane and the CBD before winding its way past Kangaroo Point and New Farm. *Opposite:* Panoramic views of Brisbane can be seen from Mt Coot-tha Lookout.

BRISBANE BY NIGHT

Between dusk and dawn, Brisbane casts off its working day appearance as the sinuous curves of the Brisbane River glow with the night lights of the city skyline. Celebratory fireworks at New Year's Eve and during the River*Festival* in September add to the city's vibrancy.

Above: CBD towers form a glittering backdrop for the Story Bridge, festooned in light. **Left:** Victoria Bridge spans the river between South Brisbane and the CBD. **Opposite:** The incendiary magic of RiverFire is an annual event.

Brisbane Style

Brisbanites enjoy a lively, cosmopolitan city where business and pleasure are pursued against a backdrop of waterfront and bushland parks. A unique blend of the old and the new give the city a simple elegance. Near the city centre, the Botanic Gardens provide both respite from city streets and the perfect venue for special events.

South Bank, across the river from the CBD, is an oasis for leisure and cultural pursuits against the backdrop of the city highrises. Picnic facilities and an award-winning boardwalk along the base of the Kangaroo Point cliffs are well utilised. On the outskirts of the city, scenic Mt Coot-tha reveals a remarkable panorama with views sweeping across the city to Moreton Bay and northward to the Glass House Mountains of the Sunshine Coast hinterland.

*This page, clockwise from top: Queenslanders – houses on stilts; relaxing in the City Botanic Gardens; Roma Street Parkland Spectacle Garden; Paniyiri Greek Festival. **Opposite, top to bottom:** Paddlewheeler river cruises leave from Eagle Street Pier; the lagoon at South Bank Parklands.*

GOLD COAST AND HINTERLAND

The Gold Coast is a 70-kilometre stretch of sun-drenched beaches, thrilling theme parks and world-class resorts, backed by a hinterland featuring subtropical rainforest, waterfalls and sweeping vistas. With sporting events such as the Magic Millions Racing Carnival and Indy 300 Motor Racing gracing the region's social calendar, it is easy to see why this glittering holiday destination attracts sunseekers and thrillseekers from around the world. For nature lovers, the beauty of the Darlington and McPherson Ranges are just a short drive away.

Above: Skyscrapers tower over the long, sandy beaches of the Gold Coast. Right: Purling Brook Falls, Springbrook National Park.
Opposite, left to right: A hinterland view of the Gold Coast; catching a late afternoon wave.

AROUND THE SUNSHINE COAST

Rocky headlands anchor a series of coves and surf beaches between Rainbow Beach and Caloundra, making up Queensland's Sunshine Coast, just north of Brisbane. Towns such as Mooloolaba, Maroochydore and Noosa are noted for their relaxed lifestyle and waterfront restaurants. Behind the coast, the hinterland contains delightful hilltop towns, fresh local produce and forested national parks. In the midst of the hinterland, the volcanic plugs of the Glass House Mountains rise dramatically above the green and fertile countryside.

Above: Looking south over Coolum. **Left, top to bottom:** Strolling the boardwalk of Main Beach, Noosa Heads; the Glass House Mountains rise above forests and farmland.

FRASER ISLAND

Take a boat from Hervey Bay to World-Heritage-listed Fraser Island, the largest sand island in the world, which supports a unique ecosystem of sand dunes, perched lakes, majestic forests and flowering heaths. Its habitats provide for more than 350 bird species and one of the few purebred populations of Dingos.

Clockwise from above: *Humpback Whales frolic in Hervey Bay; rainforest lines Wanggoolba Creek on Fraser Island; Wathumba Creek Estuary; a Dingo patrols the beach.*

THE CENTRAL COAST

The State's central coastline incorporates the Coral Coast near Bundaberg, the Discovery Coast up to Gladstone, the Capricorn Coast near Rockhampton and the stretch of magical beaches up to Townsville.

Sandy shores of the region are protected by the Great Barrier Reef, while inland numerous towns and cities service the sugar cane, beef cattle and mining industries. The cities of the central coast are also departure points for visits to reef-fringed continental islands and the Great Barrier Reef.

This page, clockwise from top left: Lady Elliot Island; Whitehaven Beach, Hill Inlet and Tongue Point, Whitsunday Island; Castle Rock and Breakwater Marina, Townsville.
Opposite, clockwise from top left: Discovering the wonders of the Great Barrier Reef Marine Park: Rose Sea Star; Long-nose Butterflyfish; Long-nose Hawkfish; diving among a school of fish; coral; Emperor Angelfish; snorkellers enjoy the underwater view; feather star; soft coral.

CAIRNS AND SURROUNDS

The laid-back city of Cairns makes an ideal base for discovering the tropical delights of hinterland rainforests and the northern section of the Great Barrier Reef. More than just a tropical tourist haven, it is also a vibrant port town for the surrounding agricultural area, and a business centre in its own right. Voted Australia's most livable regional city, its 125,000 residents enjoy the relaxed pace and outdoors lifestyle afforded by the abundance of lush gardens, parklands, beaches and waterways within the city's reaches, and the two adjacent World Heritage Areas.

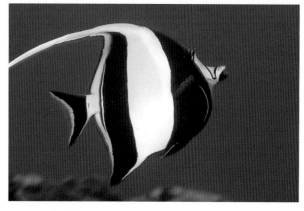

Clockwise from top: *The Lagoon on Cairns Esplanade; Cairns and Trinity Inlet; a Moorish Idol; snorkelling at Green Island; feather stars perch on a Gorgonian Sea Fan.* **Opposite, top to bottom:** *Four Mile Beach, Port Douglas; the Frankland Islands; Green Island.*

MOUNTAINS AND TABLELAND

Tropical rainforests, prime farming land and rivers plunging through deep gorges typify the area around the Great Dividing Range west of Cairns. Amongst the tableland farms from Mareeba to Herberton are intriguing volcanic formations and pockets of lush rainforest. One of the best ways to see the region is on the historic Scenic Railway, which provides breathtaking views and a sense of pioneering adventure as it winds its way past waterfalls and cliffs. The Skyrail Rainforest Cableway is an equally exhilarating option. Whether enjoying a ride high over the Wet Tropics rainforests or personally exploring it at several mid-stations, the tablelands offer a very special natural experience.

Clockwise from top right: A bird's-eye view of Cairns and the rainforest on the Skyrail Rainforest Cableway; the historic Kuranda Scenic Railway; Millaa Millaa Falls in the Atherton Tableland; whitewater rafting through Tully Gorge; Southern Cassowaries are commonly seen.

WONDROUS WILDLIFE

Thriving on the region's rich volcanic soils are World Heritage-listed rainforest and a patchwork of diverse farmlands, which combine to create the perfect environment for wildlife. Reptiles and amphibians are also well supported in this region of high rainfall, and the estuaries, creeks and swamps are home to a diversity of aquatic life.

Clockwise from top left: Boyd's Forest Dragon; Green Python; Estuarine Crocodile; Orange-eyed Tree-frog; Striped Possum.

THE DAINTREE

The Daintree, in the Wet Tropics World Heritage Area, is a hothouse of biological diversity. Here, reef-fringed beaches and mangrove forests merge with lowland rainforests that climb to the more remote highlands, blanketing the mountainous peaks.

Clockwise from far left: *A coastal forest of Fan Palms; the buttressed trunk of a rainforest tree; Rose-crowned Fruit-dove; Cairns Birdwing Butterfly.*

NORTHERN TERRITORY

The Northern Territory occupies fifteen percent of Australia, but is home to only one percent of its population. Once part of New South Wales and then South Australia, the territory came under Commonwealth control in 1911. In July 1978 it became a self-governing entity. The State's economy, founded on the grazing industry, is now supported by mining and tourism.

The Northern Territory is a land of contrasts and its two distinct faces are commonly known as the Top End and the Red Centre. It is hard to imagine two more different worlds than the vast coastal wetlands of the tropical north and the rolling red sandplains of Australia's desert heartland.

For Aborigines, the landscapes of the territory are a record of the journeys and activities of ancestral beings who shaped the land and created life. Responsibility for the well-being of the land and its life forms is maintained through a system of spiritual beliefs and cultural laws known as *Tjukurpa*.

Kakadu and Uluru-Kata Tjuta National Parks embrace two of the territory's best known landscapes and are managed jointly by Aboriginal landowners and the Commonwealth. The significance of their cultural, geological and biological features is recognised internationally and both have been designated World Heritage Areas.

Darwin, capital of the Territory stands in a magnificent natural setting, on the peninsula bounded by Frances Bay, Darwin Harbour and Fannie Bay.

Opposite: *A sunset silhouette of Pandanus trees.*
This page: *Exploring the foreshore at Nightcliff in the northern suburbs of Darwin.*

DARWIN

The city of Darwin, rebuilt after Cyclone Tracy swept through in 1974, has emerged as a modern, colourful and progressive capital city. A tropical setting and multicultural population impart a unique atmosphere to this gateway to the Top End.

Today, the Northern Territory's capital displays architectural styles and civic planning that complement its tropical climate and the relaxed lifestyle of its inhabitants.

This page, clockwise from top left: A surf lifesaver patrols Mindil Beach; bargain hunting at Mindil Markets; a bright float enlivens the Grand Parade of the festival of Darwin.
Opposite, clockwise from left: Bicentennial Park on The Esplanade; Government House; an inspired, if abstract, impression of the introduced water buffalo.

LITCHFIELD NATIONAL PARK

Sandstone escarpments, monsoon forests and lowland floodplains in Litchfield National Park are home to an impressive variety of birds, reptiles and mammals. Many of the park's walking trails lead to waterfalls or deep swimming pools that provide welcome relief from the Top End heat.

Clockwise from top: Cooling off in a plunge pool at Florence Falls; the marsupial Sugar Glider inhabits forests and woodlands; a Frilled Lizard defends itself by showing its gaping mouth and raised frill.

KAKADU NATIONAL PARK

It is humbling and inspiring to experience the beauty and spirituality of Kakadu. This outstanding World Heritage Area is famous for its sandstone and floodplain landscapes, biological diversity and Aboriginal cultural heritage. The deepwater billabongs of Kakadu are among the most fascinating of the world's ecosystems. Each wet season, torrents pour down upon the sandstone Arnhem Land plateau and cascade over the edge. Replenished billabongs spring to life and become crowded with birds, aquatic plants and animals.

***Below:** Nourlangie Rock, a sandstone outlier of the Arnhem Land plateau, reflected in Anbangbang Billabong. **Left:** The availability of water determines the six seasons of Kakadu.*

TOP END WETLANDS

The Top End's wetland habitats include rivers, sedge and paperpark swamps, billabongs, mudflats and mangroves. Monsoon rains unite these wetlands prompting an outburst of plant growth and animal activity on the floodplains.

Clockwise from left: *Black-necked Stork (Jabiru); Estuarine Crocodile; Lotus Lily; Great Egret.*

THE CYCLE OF LIFE

The wet season is a time of renewal and growth. After the rains recede and rivers resume their courses, the floodplains begin to dry and animals retreat to isolated waterholes and their dry season habitats on and around the escarpments.

Left: The South Alligator River floods across lowland plains in the wet season. ***Above:*** *As the floodplains dry out, plant life dies off.*

Arnhem Land Culture

Arnhem Land Aborigines believe that spiritual and physical connections exist between the land and all living things. Their galleries of rock art record Bininj creation beliefs over the past 30,000 years.

Left: *Anbangbang Gallery, Nourlangie Rock.* **Above:** *The late Bill Neidjie believed photographs of himself and his people's sacred art sites would foster a greater understanding of Aboriginal culture.*

THE RED CENTRE

Breathtaking in its immensity and awe-inspiring in its rugged grandeur, the Red Centre is full of marvels. Time and the elements have reduced the mountains of Central Australia to vast dunefields punctuated by sandstone monoliths and low ranges, but close inspection reveals plants and animals that are uniquely adapted to this harsh environment. More than 700 plant species have been recorded in Watarrka National Park, where Kings Canyon, Central Australia's deepest canyon, protects graceful palm trees and flora.

Clockwise from top: The sandstone domes of Kata Tjuṯa; Sturt's Desert Rose, the official floral emblem of the Northern Territory; Kings Canyon, Watarrka National Park.
Opposite: Uluṟu rises 348 metres above the sandplains.

61

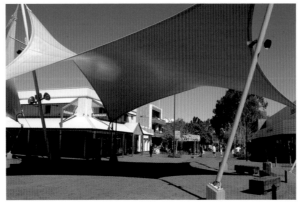

AROUND ALICE SPRINGS

Alice Springs, once a small repeater station on the overland telegraph line and then a WWII military base, is now a small, modern town made famous by Neville Shute's 1950 novel, *A Town Like Alice*. Situated slightly south of the true centre of Australia and straddled by the rugged red hills of the Macdonnell Ranges, "The Alice" is close to some of the country's most memorable scenic attractions, with Uluru, Kata Tjuta and Palm Valley all within 200 to 300 kilometres of the town.

Clockwise from top left: *Ormiston Gorge; MacDonnell Ranges; the old Telegraph Station was built in the 1870s; Alice Springs Desert Park; the excitement of the annual rodeo; Alice Springs town centre.*

SOUTH OF THE ALICE

Aspects of the desert's geological and human history
are revealed in a series of small reserves south of
Alice Springs that feature Aboriginal rock art, natural
landmarks, sandstone formations, claypans and
meteorite craters.

Above: Wildflowers edge a claypan below Rainbow Valley's
sandstone cliffs.

SOUTH AUSTRALIA

South Australia is the fourth-largest of Australia's States and Territories, and is as beautiful as it is diverse. Proclaimed a British colony in 1836, settlers eschewed the use of convict labour and were required to pay for landholdings, making South Australia the nation's first example of true colonialism.

In the 1850s, the discovery of exploitable minerals added significant wealth to a colonial economy that was based largely on agriculture and grazing. While minerals, wool and grain remain South Australia's chief exports, the State now boasts profitable wine and seafood industries.

The State's richly textured social history began with the culture of Aboriginal peoples, and continued with South Australia's history of political and social innovation. Immigrants arrived and the sharing of cultures was encouraged, helping to create today's multicultural "Festival State". South Australia's capital, Adelaide, hosts many cultural events, including the biennial Festival of Arts, the Fringe Festival, Writers Week and WOMADelaide, all of which attract national and international participants.

South Australia is also Australia's driest State and eighty percent of its landmass receives less than 400 millimetres of annual rainfall. Most of the State's population lives in the south-east, where a Mediterranean climate prevails. Beyond the Murray River's irrigated croplands and the moderating influences of coastal ranges, arable lands give way to northern deserts and the limestone-capped expanse of the Nullarbor Plain to the west.

Opposite: On Torrens Lake, the excursion launch Popeye *passes the Festival Centre.* **This page:** *The beachside suburb of Glenelg.*

ADELAIDE – CITY OF CHURCHES

Adelaide, the capital of South Australia, lies on a coastal plain between Gulf St Vincent and the Mount Lofty Ranges. The CBD retains the vision of the State's first Surveyor-General, Colonel William Light, who planned extensive parklands surrounding a central grid of wide avenues anchored by five public squares. The grand spires of Adelaide's many churches rise above the city, giving it the title "City of Churches".

Above: An aerial view across Adelaide Oval, the River Torrens and CBD to the Mount Lofty Ranges. **Left:** St Francis Xavier's Cathedral in Wakefield Street. **Opposite, bottom left:** The Stag Hotel on Rundle Street.

BEACHSIDE SUBURBS

Adelaide's golden beaches stretch southwards from Outer Harbour to the glacial deposits of Hallett Cove. Families crowd the beaches on hot summer days often lingering to watch spectacular sunsets over Gulf St Vincent.

*Above: Glenelg on Holdfast Bay was the landing site of the State's first European settlers. **Right:** Historic buildings and lighthouse at Queen's Wharf, Port Adelaide.*

THE ADELAIDE HILLS

Historic villages, wonderful local produce, formal gardens and natural bushland await those who ascend the tiered slopes of the Mount Lofty Ranges. The seasonal colours of spring flowers and autumn leaves endow the Adelaide Hills with a special beauty.

Above: One of the historic inns on Main Street, Hahndorf, established in 1863. *Right:* A display of wildflowers at Wittunga Botanic Gardens, Blackwood.

THE MID-NORTH

North of Adelaide, well-tended vineyards and orchards spread in vivid colour across the Clare and Barossa Valleys. The mid-north's old-world charm is a legacy of the European farmers and miners who settled the region.

This page top to bottom: Barossa Valley vineyards produce fine vintages; Chateau Yaldara winery; copper mining brought wealth to the town of Burra; railways have played an important role in the development of Port Pirie and the grand old Railway Station now houses a museum.

THE FLINDERS RANGES

The jagged bluffs and deep canyons of the Flinders Ranges rise above arid and grassland plains, creating a variety of wildlife habitats. Aboriginal rock art and the ruins of failed agrarian ventures record the region's cultural history.

Above: *River Red Gums mark the course of a creek that flows in the Flinders Ranges.* **Left:** *The Galah is one of more than 100 native bird species found in the region.*

KANGAROO ISLAND

Off the South Australian coast, the woodlands, heaths, wetlands and sculpted seashores of Kangaroo Island are home to an abundance of wild animals. Breeding colonies of sea-lions, fur-seals and Little Penguins can be found in some of the island's 28 protected areas.

This page, top to bottom: Western Grey Kangaroo; Australian Sea-lion. ***Opposite, clockwise from top:*** Admirals Arch, Cape du Couedic; Remarkable Rocks, Kirkpatrick Point; Cape du Couedic Lighthouse.

THE MURRAY RIVER

Australia's longest and most important waterway, the Murray River irrigates the fruit and dairy farms of Riverland towns from Renmark to Waikerie. Turning south at Morgan, it makes its final run to the sea, supplying water to Adelaide and the lakes at its mouth along the way. Until the 1890s, paddlewheelers, steamers and barges plied the river, carrying cargoes of wheat, timber, and wool. Today, "old man Murray" is an important source of irrigation for farmers and graziers. It also provides habitat for many species of native flora and fauna, especially around the Coorong wetlands.

Above right: The Murray overflows into seasonal wetlands when water levels are high. *Opposite, clockwise from top:* Paddlewheelers still operate on the river, but now carry holiday-makers instead of goods; Australian Pelicans frequent the river; Black Swans and cygnets.

TASMANIA

Tasmania, Australia's smallest and southernmost State, is a veritable Garden of Eden where the combined efforts of a maritime climate, rain-catching ranges and fertile soils clothe much of the island in lush greenery.

The "Island State" encompasses a high and massive central plateau of glacier-carved lakes and mountains. Deep river valleys cut into the plateau and separate it from smaller ranges in the east. A 3200-kilometre-long coastline surrounds the island with dramatic sea cliffs, sweeping bays, beaches, protected coves and deep natural harbours. The significance of many of these landscapes is acknowledged by their national park and World Heritage status.

Tasmania's cultural heritage precedes the last ice age. Aboriginal stone arrangements, middens and rock art sites are poignant reminders of the island's first settlers. European colonisation began with the onshore activities of sealers and whalers, followed by the establishment of English penal settlements. Free settlers soon arrived and began taming the eastern and northern regions and making use of the many natural resources found on the island.

Tasmanian industry still reaps the benefits of timber, mineral, agricultural and marine resources, but the island is perhaps best-known for its well-deserved reputation for niche-market diary and organic produce and cool climate wines.

Today, Tasmanians enjoy a slower-paced lifestyle that is reflected in the charm of their cities and towns. Every destination is a place to linger, explore and savour the uniquely Tasmanian lifestyle.

This page: Constitution Dock, Hobart. **Opposite:** *A cirque lake in the Arthur Range, Southwest National Park.*

HOBART

Hobart is one of Australia's loveliest capital cities. Life in this charming seaport revolves around its waterfront setting on the Derwent River, which was the 19th-century haunt of whale hunters and clipper shipwrights.

This page, top to bottom: Tasman Bridge; Salamanca Markets; a typical old-style house on Battery Point.
Opposite, top to bottom: Hobart spreads along the banks of the Derwent River; a winter view of Hobart, taken from nearby Mount Wellington.

THE SOUTH

Southern Tasmanian towns are proud of their history and retain many architectural reminders of colonial days. The region also boasts fertile farmlands, rainforested river valleys and stunning seashores. Mountains, rivers, lakes and ocean are all waiting to be explored, along with the continent's surviving remnants of true wilderness in the Tasmanian Wilderness World Heritage Area.

*Clockwise from top: Prion Bay and Precipitous Bluff; a tarn nestled in the majestic Arthur Range; the isthmus between South and North Bruny Islands; Richmond Bridge, established in 1825; Tahune Forest AirWalk near the Huon and Picton Rivers junction. **Opposite:** Russell Falls, Mount Field National Park.*

THE EAST COAST

Visitors to the east coast can expect to be awed by the many interesting historic sites and the outstanding scenery. Between the grim Port Arthur ruins and the fishing town of Bicheno stretch beaches, sheltered bays, jagged ranges, forested headlands and intriguing coastal rock formations.

This page clockwise from top: *The chilling ruins of Port Arthur Historic Site; the Blowhole and Rocking Rock at Bicheno; Tasman Island; fishing boats at Waub's Bay, Bicheno.* **Opposite, top to bottom:** *Wineglass Bay; bushwalkers take in the sights of the Freycinet Peninsula.*

Clockwise from top: Cradle Mountain and Dove Lake;
Common Wombats browse in the open forests, woodlands
and shrublands; Platypus are found in freshwater habitats; a
Tasmanian Devil displays its fearsome gape.

THE NORTH

Northern Tasmania has many superb wild places including the glaciated landscapes of Cradle Mountain and the central plateau. A wealth of delightful inland and coastal towns in the region service the agricultural and tourism industries.

Clockwise from above: *The mauve beauty of a lavender farm near Scottsdale; Mersey Bluff Lighthouse; Launceston, seen from Cataract Gorge on the Tamar River; one of Sheffield's famous wall murals, by artist John Lendis, decorates the Blacksmith Gallery.*

THE NORTH-WEST

Tasmania's north-western coastal towns were settled around river estuaries, creating excellent natural harbours for shipping supplies in to settlers and for carrying away the harvest of timber and mineral resources. Inland, much of the forest has given way to farms, except in the wildest areas of mountains and gorges. From Burnie, the scalloped shores of Bass Strait edge around to the wild west coast and south to where the Gordon River spills into Macquarie Harbour.

This page clockwise from top left: The Nut, Stanley; *Queenstown; the ABT Wilderness Railway runs from Queenstown to Strahan; Strahan and Macquarie Harbour.* **Opposite:** *Sunrise on the Gordon River.*

VICTORIA

Victoria may be the nation's smallest mainland State, but within its compact area are a range of adventures and experiences, all proof of the old saying that good things come in small packages.

From the rugged, snow-capped mountains of the Australian Alps to the temperate forests of the Otway Ranges, the State's 780 kilometres from east to west embrace a variety of natural landscapes.

The Murray River defines much of the State's northern border. Its headwaters rise in the Great Dividing Range, which arcs through the north-east high country before ending amid the sandstone formations of the Grampians in central Victoria. It is this unique combination of natural assets that underlies the State's economic prosperity and stability.

The discovery of gold in the 1850s brought great riches to Victoria and lured hordes of immigrants to the colony. Many remained in Victoria after the gold rush ended, contributing their skills and establishing the multiculturalism for which Victoria is still noted. A steady income from wheat, wool and timber added to the State's coffers.

Melbourne, proclaimed the State's capital in 1851, is a worthy seat of government for Victoria. It is a handsome city whose streetscapes combine 19th-century charm with the dynamism of modern architecture. As Australia's second-largest city, Melbourne is foremost a commercial centre, but its reputation for culture and the arts make it a city where quality of life and expression is also highly valued, and one whose cosmopolitan residents welcome visitors from around the world.

This page: *Werribee Park Mansion.* ***Opposite:*** *The CBD dominates the skyline above the Royal Exhibition Building.*

MELBOURNE

Melbourne, the capital of Victoria, is a cosmopolitan city renowned for fostering cultural pursuits and the arts as much as for its retail outlets, restaurants and entertainment venues. Tree-lined avenues, formal gardens and elegant stone buildings bring space and style to this commercial hub.

Above: *The Yarra River winds past sporting facilities at Melbourne Park (right) and Kings Domain, Government House and the CBD on its way to Port Phillip Bay.*
Left: *Melbourne trams with the Shrine of Remembrance beyond.* ***Opposite, bottom:*** *An afternoon paddle on the Yarra River.*

MELBOURNE BY NIGHT

Melbourne is a city that never sleeps. When the sun sets, the city turns on a dazzling display of lights, transforming the streets and beckoning people to explore and indulge in the city's numerous night-time attractions.

Clockwise from below: *The Princess Theatre; Chinatown in Collins Street; the Paris end of Collins Street; Federation Square; Flinders Street Station.* ***Opposite:*** *City towers sparkle, seen from the broad sweep of St Kilda Road.*

PORT PHILLIP BAY

Melbourne city stands approximately five kilometres from where the Yarra River enters Port Phillip Bay, but the Bay is nonetheless a focus of Melbourne living with bayside suburbs making up some of the city's most lucrative real estate. Port Phillip Bay is enclosed by the Bellarine and Mornington Peninsulas and is an ocean in miniature, its moods influenced by those of Bass Strait outside. The narrow opening between Point Lonsdale and Point Nepean is a place of swirling, sometimes dangerous currents, known as The Rip.

Clockwise from top left: Colourful bathing boxes at Brighton; the whimsical figures of Jan Mitchell's Baywalk Bollards adorn the foreshore, near Cunningham Pier, Geelong; Point Nepean, Mornington Peninsula.

EAST TO THE RANGES

Majestic hardwood forests flourish in the volcanic soils and cool, moist climate of the Dandenong and Yarra Ranges. Glorious formal gardens, bushland walking tracks and city vistas make the ranges that surround Melbourne popular weekend getaways.

Top: Scenic thrills on Puffing Billy. *Below:* Mountain Ash tower over tree ferns in the Dandenong Ranges. *Left:* The Koala is one of many native inhabitants found at Healesville Sanctuary in the Yarra Ranges.

PHILLIP ISLAND

Phillip Island, at the entrance to Western Port Bay, is a well-known holiday destination. Calm beaches on the island's Western Port side are ideal for families, while the exposed southern coastline contains some of the best surf beaches in Victoria.

Colonies of Little Penguins and Australian Fur-seals attract wildlife watchers, with the daily Penguin Parade proving a highlight. After a hard day's fishing, these flightless little birds waddle up the beach to their nests at sunset, delighting crowds of tourists. Close encounters with native creatures can also be had by taking a cruise to see Australian Fur-seals on Seal Rocks, or by visiting the island's Koala Conservation Centre.

Clockwise from left: The wild seas of Bass Strait; a parade of Little Penguins comes ashore at dusk; feeding time for Australian Pelicans at Cowes.

THE PROM AND GIPPSLAND

South-east of Melbourne, the granite headlands of Wilsons Promontory jut into Bass Strait and the Tasman Sea. This magnificent place, known as "The Prom" to locals, is resplendent with rugged cliffs, sandy beaches, flowering heathland and rainforest gullies, making it of particular appeal to naturalists and bushwalkers.

Further east are the extensive waterways that feed the Gippsland Lakes, Australia's largest system of internal waterways, which cover a distance of 60 kilometres. Lake Wellington, at the western end, connects to Lake Victoria via McLennans Strait, then flows on to Lake King, where the water passes through a human-created entrance at the tourist resort of Lakes Entrance, and out to Bass Strait.

Below: Whitewater rafting on the Mitchell River. **Right, top to bottom:** *Windswept South East Point, Wilsons Promontory; granite reflections at Whisky Bay, Wilsons Promontory.*

THE MID-WEST

From the undulating mid-west plains, the bold profile of the Grampians stands out against the sky. These sandstone ranges form craggy rockfaces and cascading creeks, and are a natural haven for an array of plants and animals. Nearby, the steep cliffs of Mount Arapiles provide a challenge even for experienced rock-climbers.

Clockwise from top left: Mackenzie Falls, the Grampians; many bird species, including the Crimson Rosella, live in the Grampians; pastures and crops spread over the plains.

THE GOLDFIELDS

The towns of Ballarat and Bendigo were at the centre of the heady days of the gold rush, bushrangers and the Eureka Stockade rebellion. The goldfield towns are proud of their history and provide tourists with a glimpse of what life was like in Victoria's golden age.

Above, top to bottom: *Gold rush times are recreated at Sovereign Hill.* ***Left:*** *Midtown Ballarat.*

Clockwise from top: *Limestone cliffs line the spectacular Shipwreck Coast; boats bob on the Moyne River at Port Fairy; Cape Otway Lighthouse was first lit in 1848; the town of Lorne, on the Great Ocean Road.*

THE SOUTH-WEST

The forests of the Otway Ranges, in Victoria's south-west reveal wonders that equal the coast's splendour – rainforest, cascading waterfalls and tall trees. But it is the seascapes along the Great Ocean Road, where wind and wave have conspired to sculpt the limestone cliffs, that most capture the imagination. Stone stacks, cut by erosion from the coast and battered by ocean waves, provide one of the world's great spectacles. This panorama of windswept beauty continues along the etched limestone cliffs of the Shipwreck Coast and sweeps to a finish on the shores of Discovery Bay.

This page, left to right: Erskine Falls plunge into rainforest near Lorne; Beauchamp Falls in the Otway Ranges.

THE MURRAY RIVER

The mighty Murray River courses along Victoria's northern boundary from the high country to the western plains. In days gone by, it represented an important source of trade; today, the wide waterway is an irrigation source for farming communities and protects diverse wetland and riverine habitats.

Top: The Murray flows near Wadonga. ***Left:*** *Exploring the upper river reaches on horseback.* ***Opposite, top and bottom right:*** *Paddlewheelers depart from Echuca on leisurely river cruises.* ***Opposite, bottom left:*** *A relaxing way to travel along the Murray River.*

THE HIGH COUNTRY

Victoria's multi-faceted high country attracts visitors throughout the year. Covered by a blanket of white in winter, in summer the Australian Alps emerge from the skiing season to invite fair-weather explorations of wildflower-carpeted meadows, flowing rivers and high plains dotted with grazing sheep and cattle.

These pages, clockwise from below: Wattles flower amid Snow Gums in the woodland; the main street of Bright; deciduous trees respond to Autumn's touch; Beechworth; the snowy peaks of Mount Hotham; hitting the slopes.

WESTERN AUSTRALIA

Western Australia extends the length of the continent and occupies about one-third of Australia's surface area. From the Joseph Bonaparte Gulf, its 12,500-kilometre-long coastline stretches to the sheer cliffs of the Great Australian Bight.

Beyond its coastal landscapes, this immense State ranges from savanna-clad sandstone plateaus in the north through the rugged ranges, semi-arid grasslands and arid deserts of the central and south-east regions. In the South-West Corner, a Mediterranean climate prevails over fertile valleys and remnant eucalypt forests.

Western Australia's human history is as diverse as its climate and landscapes. Evidence suggests the north was an entry point for Australia's first settlers, who island-hopped across a much narrower Timor Sea prior to the last ice age. Seafarers littered the coast before Captain Fremantle proclaimed the west a British colony in 1829.

The site of the Swan River settlement, originally a Nyungar meeting place, now lies at the heart of the State's capital city, Perth. Its gleaming towers of commerce are a bold reflection of Western Australia's thriving economy, which is based on vast mineral deposits and supplemented by crops, livestock and marine resources.

This page: *A floral timepiece is one of Kings Park's many botanical attractions.* **Opposite:** *Visitors to Kings Park on Mount Eliza enjoy panoramic views of Perth and the Swan River.*

PERTH

Settled in 1829 by the British, Perth truly began to prosper with the discovery of gold in 1892. Today, Perth is a prosperous and beautiful city with efficient public transport, a compact city centre, a wealth of culture and easy access to surrounding scenic regions.

These pages, clockwise from below: The Swan Bells tower holds a working peal of 18 bells; sailing boats on the Swan River; Southern Cross Fountain, John Oldham Park; the Narrows Bridge links South Perth to the CBD.

PERTH'S CITY BEACHES

Throughout the year, Perth residents enjoy the seaside attractions of silvery beaches and sheltered harbours. And there is no better finish to a great day at the beach than a glorious Indian Ocean sunset. Safe, calm waters make Perth's beaches ideal for swimming, boating and sailing.

Top: *Hillarys Boat Harbour at Sorrento.* **Centre:** *Cottesloe's patrolled beach is popular with families.* **Left:** *The ocean swell off Scarborough Beach attracts surfers and sailboarders.*

FREMANTLE

At the mouth of the Swan River is the State's largest seaport, Fremantle. Much of Fremantle's seafaring heritage is on display at the Maritime Museum, but this charming city has recently acquired a growing reputation as a centre for the arts. Fremantle is a departure point for trips to one of Perth's favourite playgrounds, Rottnest Island.

Above: Cargo ships, fishing boats and pleasure craft fill Fremantle's harbour complex. *Right:* Restored colonial buildings grace the streets of Fremantle.

THE SOUTH-WEST CORNER

Fragile sea cliffs, subterranean caves, windswept heath and tall forests are some of the scenic highlights of the South-West. The region is also well known for its award-winning Margaret River wines, and the summer influx of migratory birds that flock to the coast.

Above, top to bottom: Busselton Jetty; Vasse Felix winery at Margaret River. ***Below:*** *Cape Naturaliste Lighthouse.*
Right: *Wildlife watching from the Sugarloaf Rock lookout, Leeuwin-Naturaliste National Park.*

THE SOUTH COAST

Forests, wetlands and heaths lie behind the rugged south coastline of sculpted bays, granite headlands and dunes. Maritime, timber and farming towns of the region, from Augusta to Eucla, offer a look at times past.

Clockwise from top: *The Salmon Holes, Torndirrup National Park; Fitzgerald River National Park is a World Biosphere Reserve; the port of Albany; a female Southern Right Whale and calf.*

STIRLING RANGE

The foothills, valleys and serrated peaks of Stirling Range National Park support more than 1500 species of plants, including 123 types of ground orchids. Its wildflower displays are as spectacular as its rock-climbs and summit views. Some of the wildflower species here occur nowhere else in the world and some peaks have their own distinct wildflower populations.

Top: Stirling Range rises over 1000 metres above the cultivated plains. ***Centre, left to right:*** *Showy Dryandra; Hood-leaved Hakea.* ***Bottom, left to right:*** *Queen of Sheba Orchid; Scarlet Banksia.*

THE WHEATBELT

The central plains east of the Darling Range are Western Australia's agricultural heartland. Unusual rock formations stand amid wheatfields and pastures hemmed with spring-flowering shrubs and eucalypt trees that shelter native animals.

Clockwise from top left: *Farm dogs catch a lift to work; Wave Rock near Hyden; harvested hay is ready for storage; a tribute to the Merino wool industry at Wagin.*

THE GOLDFIELDS

The discovery of gold at Coolgardie in 1892 set Western Australia on the road to prosperity. Tales of hardship and of discovering instant wealth can be found in the region's ghost towns, museums and grand public buildings.

Clockwise from top left: The Town Hall at York; a miner's hut is a reminder of the determined people who once settled Arthur River; Edwardian-style buildings in Hannan Street, Kalgoorlie.

THE BATAVIA COAST

During the 1600s, Dutch and French navigators charted and named much of the spectacular but treacherous west coast. The region is as famous for its sandstone gorges, limestone pillars and spring wildflowers as its maritime history.

This page, top to bottom: Houtman Abrolhos is an archipelago of at least 122 coral islands; Murchison River, Kalbarri National Park; the Pinnacles, Nambung National Park; Zuytdorp Cliffs.

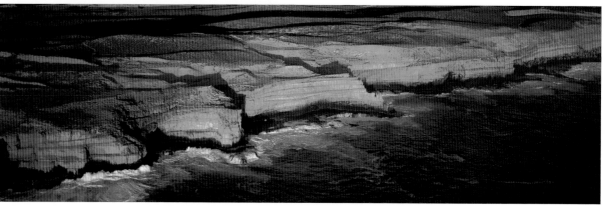

SHARK BAY

The Shark Bay World Heritage Area is a climatic crossroad where a diversity of uncommon plants and animals meet. Its marine inhabitants include Bottlenose Dolphins, Dugongs, sea turtles, and stromatolite-building micro-organisms.

Above, top to bottom: Bottlenose Dolphins are frequent visitors to Monkey Mia; coastal plains burst into flower from August to October. **Right:** The red cliffs and dunes of François Peron National Park.

THE PILBARA

Ancient landscapes of the Pilbara contain some of the country's greatest mineral deposits. While spinifex hummocks and scattered eucalypts clothe the iron-rich ranges, ferns and figs shelter in deep, damp gorges.

Clockwise from top right: *Hamersley Range, Karijini National Park; Fortescue Falls, Karijini National Park; Mount Augustus, also known as Burringurrah, is the world's largest rock.*

THE CORAL COAST

Ningaloo Reef is a 260-kilometre-long barrier of pristine coral reefs lying within sight of Cape Range National Park. It is the largest fringing coral reef in Australia and the only reef in the world found so close to a continental land mass. Itinerant Whale Sharks, Manta Rays, big game fish and Humpback Whales ply the outer edges of this coral paradise. The coral reef fish found are among the most colourful and beautifully patterned of all living creatures. Even the novice snorkeller can swim in the shallows and witness an amazing variety of fish life.

Clockwise from top: The tranquil water of the coast; Vlamingh Head Lighthouse near North West Cape; discovering marine life at Ningaloo Marine Park.

THE KIMBERLEY

The geological formation of the Kimberley is revealed in a stunning display of wide plains, fossil reefs, folded ranges and drowned valleys. Life in these undeveloped landscapes ebbs and flows under the influence of a tropical monsoon climate. The rugged country around Geikie and Windjana Gorges, the King Leopold Ranges and Purnululu National Park, harbours abundant wildlife. Birds, turtles, crocodiles, kangaroos and wallabies are just some of the many animals inhabiting this dramatic landscape.

Top to bottom: *The sandstone domes of the Bungle Bungle Range, Purnululu National Park; children at play near Broome; herding stock on the savanna grasslands.*

BROOME

The southern gateway to the Kimberley is a laid-back multicultural town that retains a colourful frontier image. Broome, in the early 1900s, was the base for thousands of divers who supplied eighty percent of the world's mother-of-pearl.

Top to bottom: Sculpted sandstone formations at Gantheaume Point; Broome's turquoise seas and pristine beaches attract winter sunseekers; a camel train traverses Cable Beach. **Pages 124–125:** Boab trees silhouetted against a dry season sunset in the Kimberley.

Published by Steve Parish Publishing Pty Ltd
PO Box 1058, Archerfield, Queensland 4108 Australia

www.steveparish.com.au

ISBN-10: 174021733 0
ISBN-13: 978174021733 0
10 9 8 7 6 5 4 3 2

Photography: Steve Parish

Additional photography: p. 96 top right: Hans & Judy Beste.

Front cover: Kata Tjuta, Uluru–Kata Tjuta National Park, Northern Territory.

Back cover, top to bottom: Hamersley Range, Karijini National Park, Western Australia; Melbourne city towers seen from St Kilda Road, Victoria; Millaa Millaa Falls, Tropical North Queensland.

Text: Cath Jones
Editing: Kate Lovett; Michele Perry & Karin Cox, SPP
Design: Cristina Pecetta & Gill Stack, SPP
Production: Tiffany Johnson, SPP
Printed in China by PrintPlus Ltd
Prepress by Colour Chiefs Digital Imaging, Brisbane, Australia

**Produced in Australia at the
Steve Parish Publishing Studios**

FOR PRODUCTS
www.steveparish.com.au

FOR LIMITED EDITION PRINTS
www.steveparishexhibits.com.au

FOR PHOTOGRAPHY EZINE
www.photographaustralia.com.au